Philosophy for children

From child to children

Once upon a time!

I0774214

The importance of daddy!

Coloring story!

By: Bernardo Octaviano Pereira

This book belongs to:

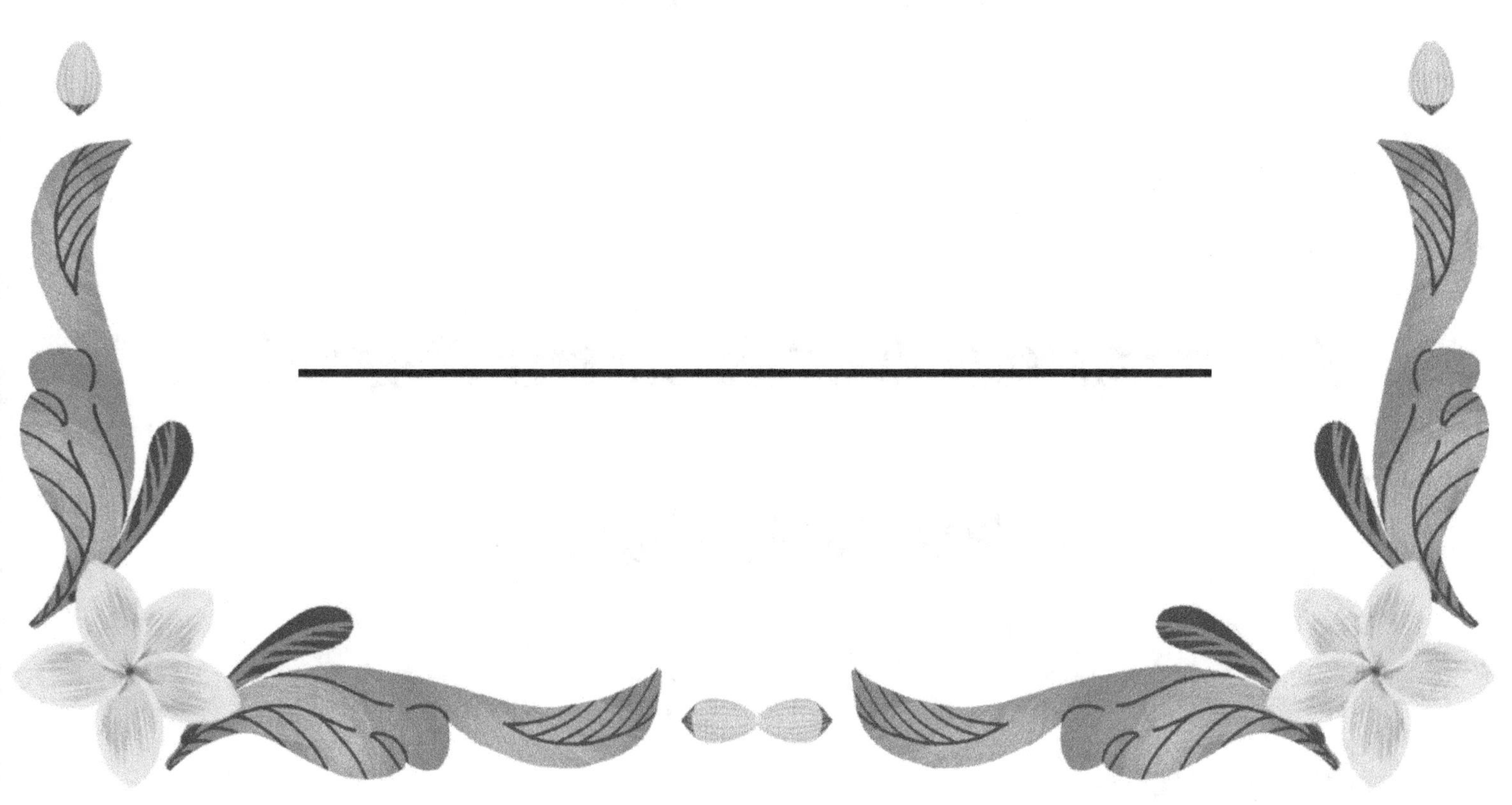

I dedicate this work, firstly, to my parents who I love so much, to my teachers, to my dear aunts and to all my friends, may God bless you all infinitely!

Bernardo Octaviano Pereira

06/04/2024

All rights reserved, no part of this book may be reproduced, in a retrieval system or transmitted in any form or by any means, whether electronic, mechanical, photocopying, recording, or otherwise, without the prior written permission of the rights holder. copyright.

@bernardo6883©

Once upon a time, in a small rural community not far from here, a father and his son walked the paths of life together.

The father, with wisdom accumulated over the years, advised his son:

Watch where you step, my son. Every step you take can shape your path.

The son, looking at his father with admiration, replied with a smile on his lips:

I watch your steps, father. Because it's your steps that I choose to follow.

These simple words captured the essence of the special bond between father and son. The son recognized his father's inspiring example and the importance of learning from his experiences and advice.

He understood that, by following in his father's footsteps, he was walking a path of wisdom, love and respect.

The father, in turn, felt his heart warmed by his son's response. He knew that his actions and words had a profound impact on his son's development and character.

With gratitude in his heart, the father continued to guide his son with love and guidance,

knowing that together they could face any challenge life threw at them.

And so, father and son continued their journey, side by side, confident that, with love,

care and
attention to
each other, they
could overcome
any obstacle
and reach great
heights
together.

Because, in the end, the union and trust between them was the basis of their success and happiness.

The end!

www.ingramcontent.com/pod-product-compliance
Lightning Source LLC
Chambersburg PA
CBHW081542250726
48659CB00009B/3046